I0821340

essential careers™

Careers in Roofing and Flooring

Daniel E. Harmon

ROSEN PUBLISHING
NEW YORK

Published in 2016 by The Rosen Publishing Group, Inc.
29 East 21st Street, New York, NY 10010

First Edition

Library of Congress Cataloging-in-Publication Data

Harmon, Daniel E., author.
Careers in roofing and flooring / Daniel E. Harmon. — First edition.
pages cm. — (Essential careers)
ISBN 978-1-4994-6213-5 (library bound)
1. Roofing—Vocational guidance—Juvenile literature. 2. Flooring—Vocational guidance—Juvenile literature. 3. Building trades—Vocational guidance—Juvenile literature. 4. Roofs—Juvenile literature. 5. Floor coverings—Juvenile literature. I. Title. II. Series: Essential careers.
TH2391.H37 2016
695.023—dc23

2015024388

Manufactured in the United States of America

contents

INTRO

A roofer glues a vinyl strip along the top of a new building. Much of a roofer's work must be done while kneeling and bending.

DUCTION

Old-timers have advice for how to weather cold and wet spells as comfortably as possible: take special care of your head and feet. That is, keep your head covered and your feet dry.

Basically, the same advice applies in the construction industry. A mistake in building a rooftop or floor can lead to dire problems. Damage to the roof or floor can put the whole building at risk. There is little room for error in any construction job—even less in roofing and flooring.

For many young people, nailing shingles on a rooftop or installing and sealing vinyl on a floor is not their idea of a career. Not only is it hard work but it seems boring. The thought of doing it daily for a living brings a frown.

An hour spent watching roofers or flooring professionals at work (from a safe distance), though, might pique their curiosity. How do roofers move so confidently and gracefully at dizzying heights while carrying and installing bulky material? How do they manage to reroof an entire house in just a day? How do flooring carpenters work so effortlessly in cramped quarters? How do tile installers produce intricate floor patterns in such a short time?

Once considered a man's job, construction today is equally open to women as a promising career field. Men and women who construct roofs and floors perform a variety of tasks. The role of helper is the most common entry point in construction. Acquiring experience and skills, helpers advance in areas of expertise—and in pay. Many begin to specialize. Flooring workers might dedicate themselves to creative projects involving mosaics or tiles. Roofers can focus on solar, garden, and other types of "green" roofing.

All new projects, including repairs and renovations of old buildings, can turn into adventures. They might involve new designs, odd—seemingly impossible—angles, difficult fittings, exotic materials, and environmentally friendly innovations. Frequently, work crews are under pressure to meet tight deadlines. Workers get to use and master a great assortment of tools that would baffle most people. (Do you know what a jamb saw is used for? A seam roller? A screed?)

There are daily challenges in properly assembling a roof or floor. No two projects are exactly the same. It might seem to unknowing observers that basic mechanical skills and strong bodies are all that's required. Much more is involved, however. Many workers undergo advanced education and training. They learn to produce intricate, artsy floor patterns and complex roof designs. Even the men and women who work on mainline construction projects are talented, well-trained professionals. All dedicated roofing and flooring workers take pride in a structure that can last for decades.

Dozens of categories of workers are engaged in roofing and flooring. This resource concentrates on roofers, carpenters, cement masons and concrete finishers, terrazzo installers and finishers, and tile and marble setters. Overall, it is a career path with excellent prospects. Roofing and flooring laborers may go on to become project managers and supervisors. They can enter related careers. Some establish their own businesses.

chapter 1

What Roofing and Flooring Professionals Do

From early times, people have sought shelter from rain and icy precipitation. Without a good cover, misery results from rain getting into shelters. Flooding and moisture can ruin food preserves and cause wooden frames and walls to rot.

Solid floors serve a similar purpose. They protect the inside of a building from groundwater. They also block the entry of pests and dangerous wildlife such as rats, snakes, and spiders.

Over the centuries, some construction workers have specialized in building roofs and floors. Living environments have changed, as have building materials. In the twenty-first century, roofing and flooring specialists are trained in advanced techniques. Some specialize in one type of building or in a particular material or construction style.

Covering a Building

Builders throughout history have learned that certain types of roofs work better than others for different structures. People in different cultures have covered their houses with the most effective materials they found available. Teepees were draped in animal hides. Prairie dwellers waterproofed roofs with layers of sod strengthened by grass. Nomads lived in tents covered

Taking careful measurements is one of a roofer's many tasks. Precise calculations are needed so that the proper amount of material is used.

mainly with animal skins; later, tents were made of canvas and synthetic fabrics. Today, roofers build and repair roofs made of asphalt shingles, sheet metal, and many other materials.

Much of the work performed by roofing professionals is simple and routine. Other tasks are complicated. The main objective is to make the roof waterproof, with no leaks. Leakage can damage a home, office, or industrial building's furnishings, appliances, and stored items. Over time, it can cause the building's framework to rot.

Before installing a new roof, the supervisor or crew chief measures the building and closely calculates how much material is necessary. Similar calculations are made in advance of roof repairs. Roofing supervisors inspect damaged roofs and determine how best to replace or repair rotten or damaged plywood subsurfaces and joists.

Depending on building requirements, a roof may have multiple layers of material. Beneath the outer shingles may be insulation or vapor barriers.

Roof workers align materials with the roof's edges and begin building the roof upward. They cut shingles or metal sheets to fit around vent openings. They caulk over nail and screw heads to prevent leaks.

Most buildings in the United States have roofs of one of four types.

LOW SLOPES

Roofs with low, or gentle, slopes have an angle of rise no greater than 3 inches (7.6 centimeters) for each foot of horizontal space. A simple roof might consist of two even sections, front and back, rising to connect in the center of the structure. If each section is 15 feet (4.6 meters) wide from edge to top, then the height in the center would be no more than 45 inches (114 cm).

Low-slope roofs typically have a single layer of waterproof material exposed to the elements. About two-thirds of buildings have low slopes. Low slopes are common on industrial and office buildings and apartment complexes.

STEEP SLOPES

Roofs featuring an angle of rise of more than 3 inches (7.6 cm) per horizontal foot are considered steep slopes. In the example above, a 15-foot-wide (4.6 m) section of roof that is higher than 45 inches (114 cm) at the top has a steep construction.

Designs that involve multiple angles present extra challenges. They can make it more precarious to balance and manipulate materials and tools.

Most steep-slope roofs are covered with shingles made of asphalt, fiberglass, metal, or wood. Single-family homes typically have steep slopes.

SUSTAINABLE ROOFS

One intriguing type of roof is built in a landscaping pattern, covered with plants. Waterproof material provides the understructure. This is covered with roots and soil, planted with various kinds of vegetation. Obviously, the substructure must be not only waterproof but also particularly sturdy. The plants require constantly moist soil, and wet sod is heavy. Sustainable roofs are uncommon but are becoming increasingly popular in modern American society.

SOLAR ROOFS

Some traditional-style roofs have solar panels inlaid. A growing number of new buildings feature dedicated solar roofs.

A solar roof serves one of three purposes. A solar reflective roof turns away the sun's heat, helping keep the building cool. A solar thermal roof absorbs sunlight for heating water. A solar photovoltaic roof also collects the sun's heat but converts it to electricity.

Most types of roofing projects usually are done by contracted crews. Crews may consist of as few as four or five laborers or as many as a dozen or more. Repair jobs might be performed by one or two carpenters.

Putting in a Solid Floor

In wooden structures, floors are constructed and repaired by carpenters. For some projects, workers with general carpentry skills can build the floor. Other projects call for the experience

The visitor center at the Brooklyn Botanic Garden features a "living rooftop." Sustainable roofs call for sturdy, waterproof understructures.

and expertise of carpenters who specialize in certain types of floor construction.

Although most wood roofing projects require crews of four or more workers, floors can be built by fewer carpenters—in some cases, just one. Many professional carpenters work for themselves. One advantage of self-employment is being able to set your own schedule. Most self-employed carpenters are contracted to build houses and housing complexes rather than commercial and industrial structures.

Most carpenters prefer to work in specific settings. Residential carpenters work on homes, condominiums, and apartment buildings. Commercial carpenters construct and remodel office buildings, schools, hospitals, malls, hotels, and other business facilities.

Carpenters who build wooden floors use blueprints and building plans. They measure and cut wood to fit the floor plan. The

A GIGANTIC UMBRELLA

How would you like to work on a stadium roof that's 115 feet (35 m) high, spans 200,000 square feet (18,581 square meters), takes two years to build, and costs $150 million? That's what hundreds of workers recently did in the Queens borough of New York City. They put a retractable roof above Arthur Ashe Stadium, the primary site of the United States Open Tennis Championships.

Arthur Ashe Stadium is the largest tennis stadium in the world, containing more than twenty-three thousand seats. Its size and location make it the ideal stadium for the U.S. Open. However, a history of inclement weather at tournament time forced U.S. Tennis Association (USTA) officials to consider options to prevent long delays in the tournament. In 2013, they authorized the building of a retractable roof—one that can be drawn away in fair weather and closed when needed. A small army of professionals labored to complete it in time for the 2016 tournament.

The roof is constructed mainly of steel and Teflon, a synthetic fiber. It is supported by twenty-four steel columns embedded as deep as 175 feet (53 m) into the ground. The deep setting is necessary because of the soft, swampy terrain beneath the stadium.

The funny thing about this multimillion-dollar roof is that USTA officials hope they'll never have to use it. They prefer that the tournament always be played in the open. The roof's only purpose is to allow the event to proceed as scheduled if it rains. Jonathan Disbrow, lead architect, told a *Wall Street Journal* reporter, "It's essentially an umbrella."

tools they use to do this include different types of electric saws and handsaws, sanders, hammers and nail guns, levels and squares, tape measures, and chisels. They use nails, screws, staples, and glues to attach boards and panels to floor structures.

Floors are made of concrete, too. Cement masons and concrete finishers have a different set of skills and use different tools. They pour, smooth, and finish floors as well as outdoor surfaces, including sidewalks and curbs. They also refinish worn floors and patch damaged floors.

Cement masons and concrete finishers construct framed sections where the floor is to be placed. They put down mesh wire or rebar, which will reinforce the concrete after it dries. Then they pour wet concrete into the sections or have it poured from concrete trucks. Finally, they spread and smooth the concrete surface. They apply waterproof sealants to protect the floor.

Concrete workers need to thoroughly understand the concreting process. Water is added to dry concrete to form a thick liquid for pouring. Workers must keep an eye on the pouring and drying process. Temperature and humidity affect how quickly the concrete dries. The floor cannot be finished until it is completely set.

FINISHING THE FLOOR

After the flooring structure is in place, workers finish the surface using whatever material the contract calls for. Many people prefer to leave their hardwood floors uncovered to display the beauty of the wood. Exposed hardwood floors are varnished or stained to protect them.

Carpet installers lay carpet onto wood or cement floors, using blocks or rolls of carpet. Before they lay the carpet, they put down a layer of padding that will make the carpeted floor comfortable to walk on. Floor finishers also are hired to put in different varieties of wood surfaces as well as linoleum, vinyl, and fake wood. Fake wood is also called engineered or

A worker puts in a hardwood floor over a subfloor made of oriented strand board (OSB). Some prefer OSB subflooring; others prefer plywood.

manufactured wood. The boards or panels are made of particles or strands of wood products held together with adhesives. Particles might include sawmill scraps, bamboo, or even vegetable fibers such as wheat straw.

On cement floors, the finish might be simply heavy coats of durable paint. It depends on the building and how it will be used. Some industrial sites and home basements have only bare concrete floors. Many commercial buildings, hospitals, government buildings, and upscale homes, on the other hand, display beautiful, elaborate flooring surfaces. These are the handiwork of terrazzo workers.

Terrazzo flooring consists of small pieces of marble, granite, or other attractive rock types, laid into a mesmerizing pattern. Terrazzo workers and finishers are not unlike artists. They create decorative interior floors, outside patios, and walkways. Like cement masons, they begin by pouring and leveling concrete surfaces. They then set to work arranging rock chips of different sizes and shapes on top. The pieces are placed into a glaze of epoxy that holds them firmly when dried. The chips and the epoxy may be of many colors, adding to the beauty of the floor.

When the epoxy has dried, the workers smooth the finish with electric grinders. They apply compounds that prepare the floor finish for future polishing.

Roofing and flooring professionals can take great pride in their work. They become experts in the use of different tools. When a project is done well, they can look down at what they've completed with satisfaction.

chapter 2

General and Specialized Careers

Workers who build the roofs and floors of homes, commercial offices, industrial plants, and skyscrapers are a diverse lot. They need different skills, depending on the structure. They work in different environments, using different materials and tools. Some work at typical construction sites. They may specialize in certain phases of a job—installing ceiling insulation or tile flooring, for example. Others specialize in modern designs such as solar roofs. Some enter related careers such as those of roofing estimators and inspectors.

The different kinds of roofing and flooring work done are generally determined by the type of building it is. Most houses have shingled roofs installed over wood frames. High-rise commercial structures and vast industrial buildings more frequently are covered by metal roofs.

Likewise, most houses have a wood-frame or concrete-slab base. You aren't likely to find a wood frame beneath a modern multistory building.

Contracting companies usually focus on one or only a few types of construction. Likewise, their workers become more experienced in building certain types of roofs or floors.

Different Roofs

Not all roofs are designed in the same way or made of the same material. Three main factors define roof types: design, material, and pitch (angle of slope).

A roofer repairs a metal roof. She is working on an A-frame, which consists of front and back sections that rise to meet at a central peak.

There are scores of roof designs. Basic examples include flat roofs, A-frames, gable roofs, gambrel roofs, and mansard roofs. There are various subcategories under each design. Some designs are particularly popular in certain regions of the country.

Roofs might be constructed of asphalt or slate shingles, wood shake, tile, and metal. Wood shake is essentially wooden shingles. It gives a roof a distinctive, historic appearance, but it usually needs more maintenance because it deteriorates faster than other shingles. Some flat roofs are made of membrane material consisting of different forms of rubber. Tile roofs—generally more expensive than other types—usually are made of clay tiles. Metals, concrete, and synthetics also are used for tiles. Metals that are used in roofing include zinc, tin, aluminum, steel, and copper.

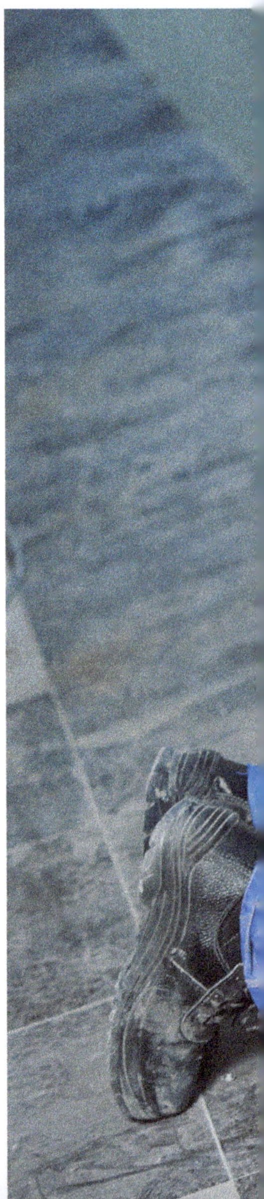

The three basic pitch angles are flat, low slope, and steep slope. The pitch of a roof is important for several reasons. It affects durability in certain weather conditions. It determines the attic space below. It also determines the kinds of draining systems that can or cannot be installed. Certain construction materials work best on certain angles of slope.

DIFFERENT FLOORS

Like roofs, floors are assembled in a variety of styles, using different materials. Workers must be knowledgeable about a material's characteristics. Many flooring workers apply themselves to one or only a few categories.

Tile and marble setters begin their task by cleaning and leveling the floor. If necessary, they make the subfloor stable with backer board or metal mesh. Then they measure and cut marble pieces and fit them into a design. Some tile and marble floor designs are quite complex. Others are simple but no less beautiful when designed and installed by experienced professionals.

Tile finishers apply grout, using a rubber trowel, to fill the spaces between pieces of tile. They wipe away the excess grout after it dries. The pieces are held in place by mortar or

A tiler repairs a floor during a renovation project. Much of the work done by flooring professionals involves existing structures that need repairs.

a different type of adhesive. Workers finish the floor by applying a sealant.

Many tile and marble flooring jobs are done in commercial buildings. Floorers often work nights and weekends so they do not disrupt office workers and their customers during regular business hours.

In some projects, laying carpet, linoleum, and vinyl flooring is done by members of a general construction crew. In others, it is performed by specially trained workers.

Green Roofing

Roofs covered with grass, flowers, and even agricultural crops are increasingly popular. They are seen especially on large high rises, government offices, and college campus buildings. Rooftop vegetation provides the building with insulation as well as basic protection from the weather. It reduces heating and air-conditioning costs. It can extend the life of a standard roof, as long as the understructure continues to be waterproof.

Green roofing work is done in basically the same environment as other roofing work. Laborers experience the same demands and challenges. However, work in green roof construction is much more complicated than ordinary roofing. These specialists install waterproof material called membranes on the roof. They then put down soil and plants, which may require irrigation. For green roof designers and installers, the work is part science and art.

Harnessing the Sun's Rays

Many young people are curious to learn how a career in roofing, flooring, or other construction work might be part of the green movement. Are certain architectural styles and building materials more fuel efficient than others? That is, can they take

Food from the Rooftop

Roofs can be more than just shelters from the elements. Since 2010, major cities worldwide have been promoting urban rooftops as gardens, farms, and meadows.

The trend began with "green roof" experiments in the late twentieth century. Environmentalists saw many benefits of rooftop greenery. Flowers and grass planted atop buildings provide excellent protection from precipitation and the sun's heat. They also provide a wildlife habitat and help purify the air.

Today, agricultural scientists encourage rooftop farming. City dwellers in the past relied entirely on produce markets for their fresh vegetables and fruits or made shopping excursions into the nearby countryside. With a garden on the roof, they can enjoy farming as a hobby and reap the harvests.

One example of rooftop farming on a large scale is Brooklyn Grange, in New York City. Its vegetable plots occupy the roofs of two city buildings. They span 2.5 acres (1 hectare). The project has expanded to set up honeybee hives on other city roofs.

A major concern for rooftop gardens is that the structure beneath be waterproof and safe from root invasion and other damage. A waterproof membrane is placed securely across the roof foundation before sod and plants are installed.

Young people who are interested in building as well as in farming might want to consider specializing in sustainable, or green, roof construction and development. This specialty may require a college degree.

advantage of natural energy sources and produce less—or no—environmental pollution? The answer is yes.

Solar tile roofs capture solar rays and convert them to usable power. Installing these roofs is a growing specialty area that

Installing solar voltaic panels atop houses and commercial buildings to harness the sun's energy is a growing specialty in the roofing industry.

might be of interest to today's teens as they consider career paths. PV (solar photovoltaic) installers are professionals who install and maintain solar panels on the roofs of houses, commercial buildings, and other structures.

Related Careers

There are interesting non-laborer jobs related to the construction industry. People in these roles include estimators, inspectors, and sales representatives.

Some of the cost estimators working in construction are construction managers. These industry veterans oversee the project's budget, organization, schedule, and actual work. Through years of experience, they can estimate with impressive accuracy what a project will cost. They place their bids accordingly.

Some large companies employ math-minded specialists whose primary job is to estimate a project's cost. The big factors to consider are materials and labor. What materials will be used? What quantity? How many workers will need to be assigned to the project and for how many hours or days? Obviously, the estimator must be intimately acquainted with roofing and flooring work.

Construction inspectors work in different areas of the industry. Generally, building inspectors examine building structures to determine quality and safety issues. Some building inspectors specialize in structural steel, for example, or in concrete. Construction inspectors are employed by contractors, property owners, insurance companies, and government agencies.

Home inspectors look at houses, condominiums and apartments, and other residential structures. They are hired by

Property owners discuss details of their new home construction with a construction manager, who works closely with them at every stage.

buyers and sellers of homes to examine the condition of a building that is being bought or sold. They point out problems or potential problems that should be resolved before the sale. Examining roofing and flooring quality is one of their most important objectives.

Large roofing and construction companies hire sales representatives to drum up new business. Many sales professionals have degrees in marketing or related subjects. A few are experienced laborers who have decided to switch to an occupation that is less physically demanding. In either case, the sales rep must have inside knowledge of roofing or flooring and an understanding of customer needs.

Roofers who have creative instincts may want to consider pursuing careers that take them beyond the physical labor. Jobs as building designers and architects require at least a bachelor's degree. Most designers of green roofs have degrees in areas such as landscape architecture or engineering. They must be knowledgeable about plant growth and nutrition, drainage, energy and water efficiency, and related subjects. Naturally, they also must be familiar with standard roof construction.

chapter 3

Required Skills and Personal Traits

Most people tend to think of roofing and flooring work as simple manual labor. Learn a few basic construction skills, find a contractor who needs laborers, start to work, and get paid.

It isn't so simple. True, most construction workers learn on the job. But they need certain natural skill sets and personal qualities. A student who is riveted to a microscope or telescope won't likely succeed in roof and floor construction. Neither will a teen whose fascination comes from figuring out how a computer game was programmed. But a young person who wants to be a builder—a builder of physical structures—is the ideal candidate for this career.

Job Basics

Mechanical aptitude is important, whether working on top of a building or at ground level. Basic skills for roofing and flooring can be

learned in trade school classes and developed on the job. Apprentices and helpers learn to work with hand and power tools. Supervisors and carpenters work with construction plans and blueprints.

Tiles are placed conveniently for workers in roofing projects. Carrying materials is usually a task given to construction helpers or apprentices.

Roofing is done outdoors, often in severe heat. In northern zones, summer is the peak season for roofing because harsh winter weather makes for sporadic building schedules. Roofers typically work long hours to complete jobs as quickly as possible, especially when rain is forecast. They frequently have to work overtime.

Obviously, roofers must be unafraid of heights. They must have good balance and equilibrium. The injury rate for roofers is higher than for most careers. Most injuries result from slips and falls from roofs, ladders, and scaffolds. Workers sometimes suffer burns from construction material such as asphalt and bitumen heated by the sun. They encounter wasps, which commonly build nests under the eaves of buildings. Foot punctures by unnoticed, exposed nail points are common. A constant awareness of safety threats is vital.

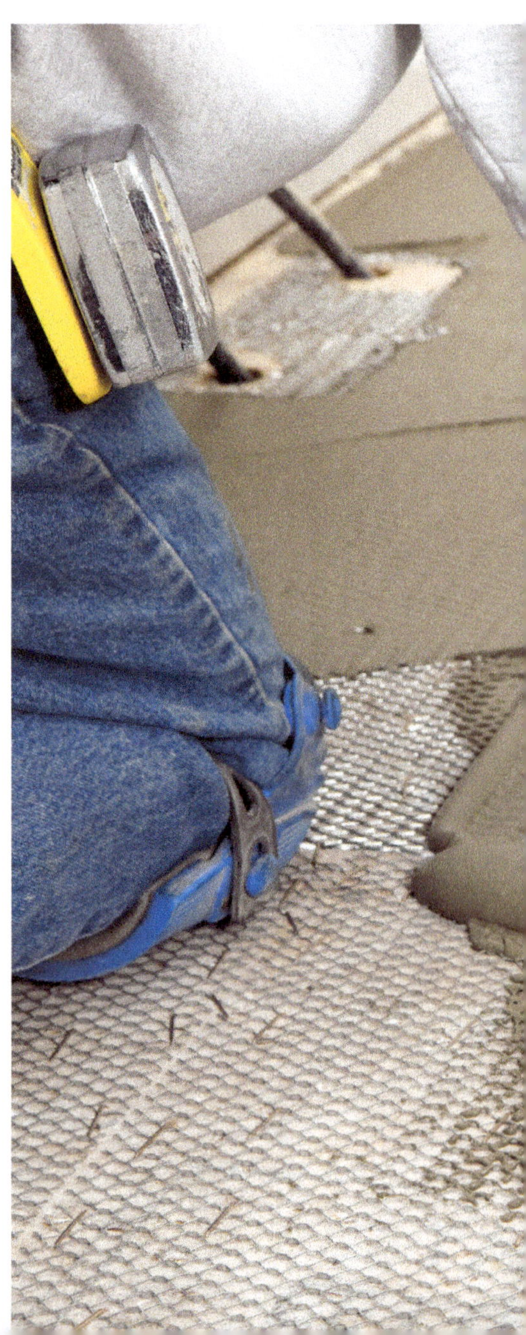

Roofers must have physical strength for lifting and carrying boards, bundles of shingles, and tools. Bulky materials may weigh more than 50 pounds (22.7 kilograms). The work involves a routine of constant bending, squatting, kneeling, and climbing. Though roof construction rarely is done in rain or severe cold, emergency repairs may be needed in any kind of weather.

Flooring carpenters are usually under less overall time stress than roofers but are expected to complete their projects on schedule. Most flooring carpenters work full-time.

A tile setter trowels mortar onto a mesh subfloor. Much of the job is performed on hands and knees. Notice the worker's use of kneepads.

A WONDERFUL WORLD OF ROOFS

For roofing professionals, many projects are routine. Others are challenging. A few are extreme. Roofs are built in a rich, fascinating variety. They account for much of the distinguishing visual character of a community, city, or region.

In the United States alone, scores of roof styles and shapes can be seen within the radius of a few miles. Here are only a few examples.

- Flat roofs. These naturally are the simplest because they have no angled sections. There are different types of flat roofs over homes, skyscrapers, and industrial buildings. They are made of different materials to serve different purposes. Although they are flat, they are not level. They must be gently tilted, or pitched, to allow rainwater runoff.
- A-frames. Two flat surfaces are joined at the top, in the shape of an inverted V. Some A-frames have wide, gentle slopes. Others are very steep.
- Arched roofs. These are rounded, like the side of a barrel.
- Gambrel roofs. While A-frames consist of one simple surface on each side, each half of a gambrel roof is divided into two sections. The upper section is steeper than the lower.
- Hip roofs. These have two primary surfaces, like A-frames. But they also have smaller angled surfaces at each end.
- Mansard roofs. Like hip roofs, they have broad side surfaces and smaller end surfaces. Like gambrel roofs, each surface is angled into two sections.
- Saw-tooth roofs. You might envision a saw-tooth roof as a series of adjoining A-frames covering one structure. In modern designs, each component may feature a steep slope on one side and a longer, gentler slope on the other.

Look online to see images of these and other roof designs. See, for example, the website for the TV show *This Old House* (http://www.thisoldhouse.com/toh/photos/0,,1213138,00.html) and Roofpedia (http://roofpedia.com/roof-types).

Busy scheduling demands may result in late hours and even weekend work.

The daily routines of flooring professionals are different from those of roofers but are no less demanding. They, too, find themselves constantly bending, kneeling, and lifting bulky, heavy building materials. On some projects, they have to maneuver in tight spaces. They don't face the daunting dangers of working in high places. However, they must be careful to avoid injuries with their cutting devices and other tools.

The same is true of those working in cement masonry, concrete finishing, and tile and marble installation. Much of the work is done while kneeling or bending and requires physical stamina. Kneepads provide some relief. Safety goggles protect the eyes when using saws, sanders, and other tools that produce flying particles.

Personal Characteristics

Do you find satisfaction driving a nail with a hammer straight into its place? Would you be interested in mastering an electrical tool that would allow you to perform that task much faster? Do you like to see things arranged in perfect, measured alignment? Are you willing to take time to measure, cut, and place the elements perfectly? If so, this kind of job could be just right for you.

Are you sloppy, tending to put things in careless order (if in any order at all)? Does physical labor make you frown? Do you hate getting on your knees to perform minor tasks? Do you get queasy looking down from high places? Then you probably won't be happy in this line of work.

The U.S. Bureau of Labor Statistics' *Occupational Outlook Handbook* (*OOH*) describes important qualities for carpenters. They include the following.

- **Manual dexterity.** Carpenters must have good hand-eye coordination in order to work effectively and safely with different tools. For a simple example, one's hammer consistently must strike the head of a nail to avoid damaging the wood.
- **Attention to detail.** Constructing a roof or floor requires precise measuring and cutting.
- **Physical strength and stamina.** Some materials that carpenters work with are heavy. A sheet of plywood, for instance, can weigh as much as 100 pounds (45 kg). Carpenters also work with heavy tools for extended periods while bending or standing on ladders.
- **Problem-solving skills.** Roofs and floors may be framed imperfectly, which means adjustments must be made in measuring, cutting, and angling some boards.
- **Math skills.** Carpenters calculate how much material is needed for a project and make frequent measurements.
- **Business skills.** A self-employed roofer or flooring worker has to figure out timelines for the work and schedules that can be kept to, keep track of hours and costs, and make wise bids on new projects.

The *OOH* points out that some of the same traits are required for cement and terrazzo workers, especially physical strength and

Roofing is not a career for those who are afraid of heights. Here, a framing contractor works on the rafters of a new building.

stamina. They constantly bend and kneel at floor level, often in dirty or muddy locations. Also, terrazzo workers need good color vision. Many of the patterns they create will consist of materials of many colors. They must create an attractive color blend.

Successful tile and marble setters possess essentially the same personal characteristics. They, too, must be physically fit because they frequently lift heavy materials and spend hours at a time working on their knees. They must be detail oriented and have excellent color vision. They must be courteous to customers and considerate of property when working inside a home.

Construction laborers and helpers also must have good physical stamina and strength. They need mechanical skills to operate and service equipment. They should be good at basic math because they help make measurements and other calculations at job sites.

Beginning a Career

Many young people begin their careers in roofing and flooring as construction laborers and helpers. The tasks they perform at construction sites require more strength and stamina than skill. Some are simple and fairly easy. Others are difficult and, at times, dangerous.

A frequent routine of laborers and helpers is carrying materials and tools for the installers on their construction teams. They load and unload lumber, shingles, and other materials onto and from trucks. They help prepare for construction by digging holes and trenches. Cement masons employ helpers to move and set the molds that will shape the wet concrete for drying.

For some of this work, laborers and helpers learn to operate and maintain special machines and equipment. Tools range from brooms and shovels to jackhammers and surveying instruments.

A worker breaks up old concrete flooring with an electric drill hammer. Construction workers learn to use a wide array of tools.

Laborers also clean up construction sites. This often involves removing boards with exposed nail tips and other hazardous materials. They dispose of waste according to building regulations.

While performing this basic work, laborers and helpers follow instructions from supervisors and experienced carpenters, roofers, masons, and other professionals. In this way, they learn about construction projects literally from the ground up. They learn to follow construction plans. They observe and assist in numerous construction tasks.

Like the professional roofers they work with, helpers and laborers sometimes work at precarious heights. Flooring assistants may be required to function in cramped spaces. They must learn safety precautions and wear necessary protective gear.

The rate of injuries for construction laborers is quite high. Injuries include cuts and burns. They also result from falls from scaffolds and ladders. Muscle strains from heavy lifting are common.

Helpers also undergo stringent physical demands. The rate of injuries among construction helpers, though, is not as high as for laborers.

Obviously, young people interested in a roofing or flooring career must be willing to work hard. They should have basic mechanical abilities and be eager to learn to work with different tools. They should be prepared to work in difficult places and understand the importance of paying careful attention to safety.

chapter 4

Education and Training

In general, carpenters and flooring professionals need more education and skill development than roofers. They have more detailed responsibilities. In roofing projects, the construction manager handles most of those details. Roofers perform the manual labor.

How to Become a Roofer

Most roofers learn their trade by doing it. Not even a high school diploma is required. On-the-job training is most important. However, even entry-level roofers must know the fundamentals of the trade. They also must understand the importance of safety on the job.

When they start work, new roofers learn from veterans. Experienced workers show them how to put material in place with various tools and equipment. At first, helpers might be asked simply to carry material and equipment and help erect scaffolds, while observing how the veterans work. But in a few weeks or months, they find themselves measuring, cutting, and fitting materials on the roof. Soon, they may be involved in laying shingles.

High schools offer courses in basic shop and carpentry. They also provide instruction in specific subjects that will equip the student with greater skills and lead to advancement potential. Related subjects include math, mechanical drawing, and blueprint reading.

A roofing apprentice learns how to work with tile. While developing skills, workers become mindful of potential hazards and the need for safety.

Mechanical drawings show diagrams of how the various parts of a construction project are to be laid out and connected. These construction components include heating, air-conditioning, and ventilation systems that will operate within the overall building structure. The structure, of course, includes floors, ceilings, and roofs.

These mechanical drawings are vital to the preparation process. Not only do they form the basis of construction but they also are important for determining how much the construction will cost. They are necessary in order for the builder to obtain a building permit from the city or county government.

Blueprints are based on the mechanical, or technical, drawings developed by architects or design engineers. A blueprint basically is a "map" of the building that is to be constructed, floor by floor. It is quite detailed, with precise measurements along walls, door and window frames, and stairs and other vertical structures.

Modern-Day Tools of the Trade

In times past, builders constructed roofs using only basic carpentry tools—hammers, saws, hand drills, levels, and yardsticks. Most of those essentials remain in today's toolboxes. But modern roofing tools include dozens of additional implements for working with wood and other roofing materials. They make it possible to do the job faster, better, and safer.

Roof carpenters use nail guns, electric saws and handsaws, mallets, electric or cordless drills, and utility knives or heavy-duty scissors for cutting soft material such as tar paper and shingles. Pop-rivet guns are used to attach sheet metal. With caulking guns, workers apply caulk around chimneys and other openings to prevent leaks. After a job is completed, they use magnet sweepers to pick up stray nails. Clean-up tools also include high-pressure blowers, vacuums, and washers.

Other tools are needed for roof replacements. Removing the old roof requires pry bars to remove boards and spud bars for scraping away deteriorating material. Workers use gas-powered or electric cutters and hatchets to divide large sections of roofing into manageable pieces for disposal.

Some of the tools needed for putting down hardwood floors are the same as those used in other areas of carpentry. Flooring workers use different types of saws—miter saws, jigsaws, jamb saws, table saws, and circular saws, among others. A special instrument called a toe kick saw is used to cut flooring material away from walls, cabinets, and doors. Workers use pull bars, nail guns, heavy-duty staplers, routers, edgers, trowels, and a variety of glues and other adhesives. A hygrometer is used to measure humidity. Excessive moisture can lead to floor problems, so the humidity must be measured before work can begin (and carpenters usually keep an eye on humidity measurements throughout the project). Floor jacks ensure a tight installation.

Concrete finishing tools include trowels, edgers, groovers, floats, screeds, and grinders. Vinyl flooring tools include a carpenter's square, tape measure, heavy roller, and vinyl cutter. Carpenters who work on floors use special cutters, jamb saws, carpet pullers, heating irons, seam rollers, wall trimmers, and other tools.

Workers who do the physical labor rarely need to see the blueprint. The project supervisor lays out the work for them.

Some green roof installers learn most of what they need to know on the job. Certain organizations that promote environmentally friendly construction offer classes in green roof installation. For other special roofing projects such as solar tiling, advanced training, skills, and knowledge are required. It may take several years to become a roofing specialist.

LEARNING TO CONSTRUCT A FLOOR

Building a floor requires carpentry skills and/or skills in concrete finishing and cement masonry. Installation of certain floor surfaces might require other specialized skills. With large construction companies, both fundamental and advanced skills might be taught through apprentice programs. New workers learn on the job, but they should prepare by taking trade school classes while in school.

Most jobs in carpentry require a high school diploma or equivalent. No particular educational requirements are needed to find jobs as cement masons or concrete finishers. Employers of terrazzo workers prefer applicants with a high school diploma.

Many terrazzo workers and concrete finishers begin their careers as construction laborers and helpers. They then enter an apprenticeship. In on-the-job training, they begin with uncomplicated chores: edging, using a straightedge on wet concrete, and jointing. Experienced workers teach them to use a variety of tools and machines. Gradually, the apprentices work faster and are given more advanced tasks.

Skills in installing specialty flooring are acquired on the job or through technical courses. No specific educational level is required for tile and marble setters, although most have high school diplomas. They begin as helpers and learn from veteran laborers. A technical school may offer instruction for specialty occupations. A few tile and marble setters become specialists in a particular product, with training provided by the manufacturer.

In high school, students interested in this kind of work can prepare themselves in shop courses. They should apply themselves in math, mechanical drawing, and related subjects such as blueprint reading, if these are offered. Shop classes, of course, can be beneficial for roofing jobs as well.

After high school, technical school credits and the completion of an apprenticeship may lead to more opportunities and higher pay when the worker begins a regular job. To advance eventually to supervisor or business owner, technical school classes in business management will be useful both for roofing and flooring careers. Students might consider taking degrees in business, engineering, or a major related to the construction industry.

Apprentices

Some roofers and carpenters begin their careers as untrained helpers. They work and learn on the job, earning entry-level pay. Meanwhile, in some parts of the country, aspiring roofers

A terrazzo worker finishes a slab of flooring made of recycled glass. The use of recycled substances to make floors is an example of green construction.

and carpenters undergo an apprenticeship that may last as long as four years.

Apprentices and helpers learn their trades by working alongside experienced laborers. Unions and contractor associations

A roofing company's safety director gives tips on fall protection as part of OSHA's National Safety Stand-Down initiative to reduce workplace falls.

sponsor apprenticeships for young people. Basic requirements are that they be at least eighteen years old, have a high school diploma or equivalent, be a United States citizen or legal resident, be physically able to perform necessary tasks, and pass a drug abuse screening.

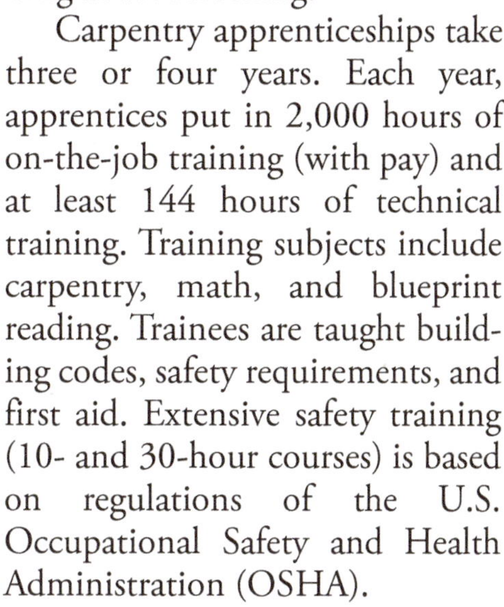

Carpentry apprenticeships take three or four years. Each year, apprentices put in 2,000 hours of on-the-job training (with pay) and at least 144 hours of technical training. Training subjects include carpentry, math, and blueprint reading. Trainees are taught building codes, safety requirements, and first aid. Extensive safety training (10- and 30-hour courses) is based on regulations of the U.S. Occupational Safety and Health Administration (OSHA).

In addition to carpentry, they learn about other construction areas including scaffold building, concrete working, welding, and rigging. The apprentices learn to work efficiently in confined spaces and to protect themselves against injuries.

Roofing apprentices learn the basics of construction and blueprint reading. This requires good math skills. Apprentices also are taught safety principles and elementary first aid. They learn to recognize hazards in their

Multicolored parquet hardwood tiles display an elaborate and gorgeous inlay pattern for flooring.

surroundings and understand the importance of the "safety first" rule. Apprentices learn the building code requirements of their cities, counties, and states. Code violations can cost them their jobs and result in serious problems for their employers.

Carpentry apprentices who complete their training become journey workers. That means they are competent to perform projects themselves.

Students who decide to make carpentry their profession might consider obtaining a two-year associate's degree. Some technical schools partner with contractor associations or trade unions to offer carpentry degree programs. Apprentices may be able to apply their training credits to their degree requirements.

Students can find information about apprenticeships at their state employment or apprenticeship agency. The U.S. Department of Labor offers information at its Employment and Training Administration website (http://www.doleta.gov) or via its help line at (877) 872-5627. In addition, apprenticeship seekers can contact construction firms or independent contractors in their areas. Some states have local union-management apprenticeship committees. These are collaborations between labor unions and companies to train workers for in-demand work.

chapter 5

Job Searching and Advancement

It's easy for some teens to find part-time jobs with roofing and other construction crews. For example, a cousin, neighbor, or family friend might be a construction supervisor who is short of workers for a project that needs to be completed right away. If the young person has manual dexterity and stamina, he or she may find Saturday employment as a helper. That early experience certainly won't hurt when looking for full-time work later.

Any work experience during your school years is important for landing your first full-time job. This is true in all career fields.

First Step: Develop a Résumé

A résumé is also known as a curriculum vitae, meaning the "course of one's life." It is a record of one's educational background, employment history, job skills, employment objectives, special interests, career goals, contact information, and references. References are former employers and others who can recommend one when applying for new jobs.

A résumé may not be required to sign on with a roofing crew. Every job seeker, though, should have one. Even students who have not held a job yet can start a résumé. The beginning

Students today can download résumé templates, research job requirements online, and review job boards and company websites for openings.

résumé can begin with basic personal and contact information. It can contain notes on the student's career interests and school courses that have helped prepare for a specific career. Any volunteer work can be listed, including productive time spent performing tasks that are not directly related to the primary career category. Likewise, any type of after-school or weekend employment (lawn mowing and other yard work, small repair tasks, and so on) should go in the résumé.

When applying for a job in writing or online, the résumé must be accompanied by a cover letter. A cover letter is a short letter of introduction explaining the applicant's interest in a particular job.

Smart professionals update their résumés often. New information includes job changes, new references, notable accomplishments, and awards and other special recognition. Contact details must be kept up-to-date.

Students can find résumé and cover letter templates, ideas, and writing advice at numerous sites on the Internet. Effective search terms include "resume," "resume tips," "winning resumes," "powerful resumes," "resume sample," and "resume template."

Résumé preparation services are available for a fee. However, with a little research and effort, most students can draft their résumés themselves.

Searching for Jobs in Your Area

Roofers seeking employment frequently get jobs through personal referrals. Company owners and supervisors learn of prospective new crewmembers from those they have already hired. Job hunters may also hear of potential openings from friends or relatives who work for a roofing contractor.

Job seekers should look up local contractors and companies who may be hiring. Prospective employers include general

Making a quick phone call to a specific construction company can disclose whether it currently is hiring and its application process.

contractors as well as roofing and flooring specialists. For best results, the job search should be organized. From the Yellow Pages and online searches, compile a list of possible employers. Some have websites containing employment information and links for applying online. Others can be contacted by letter. A simple phone call can reveal whether the firm is hiring at present. If so, the applicant may be invited to appear in person or submit a résumé.

In addition, searchers should keep an eye on local employment advertisements. These appear in the pages of newspaper classified ads. Employers also advertise online. Some job banks are free; it costs nothing for an employer to advertise and nothing for a job seeker to search for openings.

Many job-hunting websites are available. Among the most popular are CareerBuilder and Monster. Job seekers post their résumés and receive notifications of prospective jobs. Also, countless job boards are online—more than 50,000, according to *What Color Is Your Parachute? Guide to Job-Hunting Online*. The authors observe, though, that most of them are unhelpful to local job searchers.

Another way workers find new jobs and advance in their careers is by online connections. Through popular social networking platforms like Facebook and Twitter, they let it be known that they are looking for work. A dedicated career development platform for professionals is LinkedIn. Members create profiles for themselves similar to résumés. They then accumulate connections with other LinkedIn members. LinkedIn members share job leads, information, and tips.

Some construction contractors and companies are interested only in serious job applicants who likely will be with them for a long time. A steady turnover rate means they must spend more time training new workers and making them part of a team. One major roofing company with locations in different cities states on the employment page of its website: "If you're looking for a career, not just a job, and would like to be considered for future employment opportunities, send us your résumé and information."

FINDING JOB LISTINGS ONLINE

When you search for entry-level roofing and flooring positions on the Internet, you probably will be confronted with confusing advertisements. Many of the top search result listings are "sponsored" ads. Companies pay for these to appear in your search results. Sometimes when you click on one of

Starting Your Own Business

For many construction employees, the ultimate career goal is running a business. Obviously, an aspiring business owner needs to know the business inside and out. That requires years of experience. A contractor who focuses on roofing or flooring must be intimately familiar with other aspects of construction. Additionally, business owners must have outgoing personalities and good communication skills to satisfy customers.

Starting a business is no simple matter. It takes careful planning and advice from many business professionals, including a lawyer, banker, tax specialist, and insurance representative. It also requires close cooperation with government agencies that establish and monitor building regulations.

The main requirements to fulfill are as follows.

- Obtain financing.
- Become licensed and bonded and obtain necessary permits.
- Buy insurance.
- Develop a safety plan for employees that meets government requirements.
- Find top-notch laborers.
- Market the business.
- A key resource for workers interested in forming a construction business is the U.S. Small Business Administration (www.sba.gov). It provides guidelines and pointers to outside sources.

those search results, you have to dig deep to find a job opening that is in your locale and that actually is related to roofing or flooring.

Spend some time, and you eventually will locate the specific kinds of job posts you want to see. Here are some examples of results from Google searches for jobs pertaining to roofing and flooring. They have been shortened and edited from the actual listings.

- Roofer Helper. The entry-level roofer works under the direct supervision of a qualified journeyman commercial roofer, learning to install different types of roofing systems such as TPO, PVC, EPDM rubber, built-ups, bitumen, metal, and Duro-Last roofing. Additional responsibilities: checking to ensure that completed roofs are watertight; sweeping and cleaning roofs to prepare them for the application of new roofing materials; locating worn or torn areas in roofs; covering roofs with layers of roofing felt or asphalt strips before installing tile, slate, or composition material; removing old roofing materials; unloading materials and tools from the work truck; unrolling roofing; placing tiles, nailing them to roof boards and covering nail heads with roofing cement. Requires an ability to comprehend, construct, and interpret diagrams, blueprints, and shop drawings; experience working with equipment such as boom lifts, scissor lifts, and forklifts a plus; a strong working knowledge of job site safety and ability to complete a company-specific safety orientation; drug-free at all times.
- Roofing Laborer/Roofer. A commercial roofing company is currently seeking roof installers. Must have own transportation, a valid driver's license, phone, and be reliable and willing to work. Training provided. Good starting pay based on experience.
- Need Flooring Professional [an advertisement placed by a homeowner]. Work needed: complete

refinishing. Project scope: entire floor level. Approximate square footage: 500–1,000. Additional project attributes: room(s) not in a rectangular or square shape. Current flooring: solid wood, engineered wood, bamboo, laminate, and other.

- Apprentice-Level Carpenters. The apprentice will work directly under the supervision of a journeyman carpenter to construct, erect, install, and repair structures and fixtures of wood, plywood, and so on, using carpenters' hand and power tools, while conforming to local building codes. Responsibilities: helping install foundations, walls, floors, ceilings,

A construction foreman directs a crew repairing the roof of a building damaged by a hurricane in Florida.

and roofs using materials such as wood, metal, steel, plastics, and composites; erecting scaffolding; positioning and holding materials in place for installation and cutting; selecting tools and materials; cleaning work sites and equipment; cutting lumber and/or paneling to exact dimensions and drilling holes in the wood; smoothing or sanding wood surfaces.

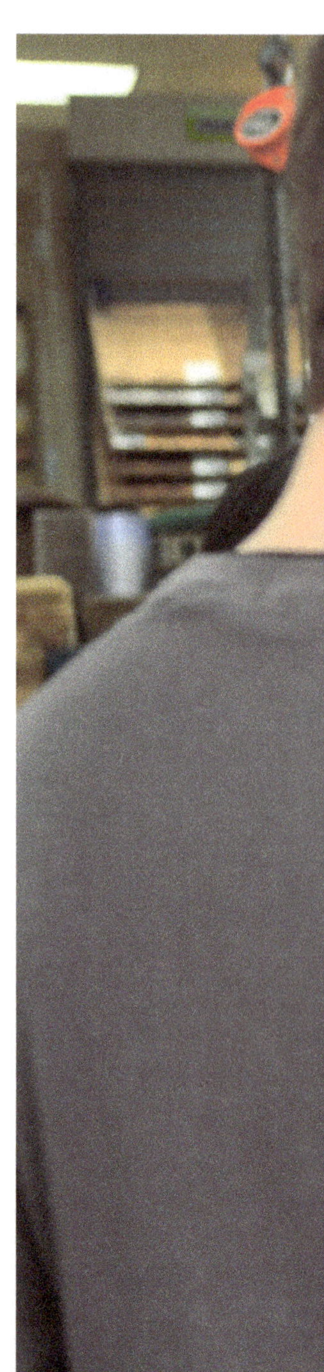

- Roofing Foreman. Responsibilities: Assist tradespersons in construction activities; conduct roof inspections as required; lead a team of roofing laborers to complete projects; load and unload construction materials; operate construction equipment; remove rubble and debris with shovels and other equipment. Education: high school diploma (or equivalent). Qualifications: previous experience in roofing, valid state driver's license, previous experience as a foreman; must be able to pass a background check.
- Commercial Roofing Sales/Estimator. Seeking an experienced roofing estimator. Applicants should have experience with estimating commercial roofing work including BUR/modifieds, single-ply, and steep slope. Must have excellent computer skills and be a team player.
- Flooring Sales Professional. Established flooring company is seeking a motivated sales professional. Some

experience requested. Excellent pay, benefits, and a company vehicle. Complete support and a beautiful showroom.

A sales representative, who must know about the characteristics of various materials, helps a customer select flooring in a home design showroom.

GETTING AHEAD

Advancement in wood construction careers is most promising for carpenters who have experience in different types of construction. Many of them eventually become construction company supervisors or self-employed, independent contractors. Some oversee all phases of a project—constructing a building from ground to rooftop. Others specialize in one phase such as framing, flooring, or roofing.

In addition to on-the-job training, carpenters can learn more about their profession through continuing education. Courses and classes in specific aspects of carpentry are provided by technical colleges, trade associations, and unions.

Carpenters interested in becoming supervisors or independent contractors can benefit greatly from learning Spanish. Many construction workers speak Spanish as their primary language.

chapter 6

A Promising Career Field

The Bureau of Labor Statistics (BLS) projects that the annual growth rate of roofing jobs will average 11 percent between now and 2022. This is approximately the average expected growth rate among all job categories in the United States.

Roofing workers hold an advantage over workers in many other careers, however: constant demand for their skills. There

The skyline of a residential community under construction indicates a diversity of roofing designs that will require professionals with many skills.

always will be jobs for roofers. Roofs are the area of a building most vulnerable to damaging forces of nature. They deteriorate faster than walls and floors. They are exposed to severe weather—hail, strong winds that fell trees and limbs, ice storms, and prolonged spells of extreme heat. According to a survey by the National Roofing Contractors Association, approximately two-thirds of roofing projects are replacements and repairs. Workers are needed to repair hail and other storm damage. They also replace rotting outer surfaces and substructures.

New construction will mean additional jobs for roofers. The BLS points out, though, that some roofing tasks will be performed by general carpenters and other construction workers. This will affect the growth rate of jobs for roofing specialists. The bureau also notes that the construction industry undergoes economic downturns. This means some roofing workers will experience times of unemployment.

A factor that will add to an uptick in jobs is the changing workforce. Workers regularly retire or switch to other occupations. This is especially true in roofing, where the work is more physically demanding and hazardous than other types of carpentry. Many laborers work as roofers only until they can find other construction jobs. These constant vacancies in the labor pool are openings for new roofers.

The growth rate in carpentry jobs is expected to be much higher—24 percent—than for roofing jobs. As in roofing, carpenters who specialize in flooring perform repairs and replacements as well as constructing new floors.

In recent years, new home construction has been vigorous following a serious downturn in the housing market. The need for carpenters is expected to continue at an above-average rate of growth. Yet, ups and downs in the economy strongly impact the building industry. The industry experiences times of high demand when there are not enough carpenters available. There are other times of slow demand when many carpenters are unemployed.

Some roofing work today is performed not on top of exposed buildings but indoors, such as installing shingles at a modular home factory.

Even in slow times, carpenters—especially those who work on floors—always will be needed for repairs and remodeling. A sagging economy may force building owners to postpone remodeling, but floor damage must be repaired promptly or it will worsen.

The demand for construction laborers and helpers is expected to grow 25 percent between now and 2022. This is much faster growth than for most occupations. Not all of these workers are engaged in roofing and flooring projects. Besides building construction, this class of laborers and helpers includes those hired to work on roads, bridges, water lines,

THE AMUSING SIDE OF ROOFING AND FLOORING

Roofing and flooring contractors have thousands of interesting stories to share about their work crews—and themselves. Some are comical, some dramatic. Many stories are both comical and dramatic. Here are real-life examples.

- A novice roofer bet his foreman that he could nail shingles faster by hand than with a pneumatic nail gun (powered by air pressure). The young person lost the bet.
- A worker on a repair job located a "soft spot" in an aging roof. Soft spots suggest rotting and weakening of the wood beneath the surface. When the homeowner arrived, the roofing foreman pointed out the weak spot. He demonstrated by lightly bouncing on it. A moment later, the dazed foreman was picking himself up from the kitchen floor below.
- Two workers came up with a plan to make their task of shingling a roof go faster. It was a method of teamwork that seemed to make sense. One took a new shingle from the pile of materials and positioned it on the roof. When he had it neatly in place, he told his partner to "shoot" it with the nail gun. Their system worked smoothly at first. Then the placer made a painful mistake. He noticed that a shingle he had just placed needed an adjustment and so he moved it—a split second after he had called, "Shoot!" The result: his hand was nailed to the roof.
- New workers sometimes misunderstand instructions. In one instance, a helper was asked to bring up a supply of 12-inch (30-cm) felt strips. What the foreman wanted was a pile of foot-long strips. What the helper delivered was a pile of uncut strips, 12 inches wide and three times too long.

- A flooring contractor was invited to inspect the handiwork of a friend who was building his own house. His friend was a proud do-it-yourselfer. When the building professional arrived, he immediately noticed a serious problem. He made a quick laser measurement. It showed the concrete foundation was slanted almost six inches (15 cm) out of level from one side to the other. There were two additional problems. First, the basement floor concrete was lumpy, not smooth. Second, the handyman had not created openings for plumbing pipes. Pipes need to be installed beneath a concrete basement floor. Repairing the mistakes was quite costly.

and other projects. Workers with the most skills will be in greatest demand.

A trend that will affect roofing and flooring careers is the increased popularity of prefabricated buildings and sections of buildings. Many roofs are now assembled in factories, then simply installed by carpenters at the building site.

Job growth is expected to be exceptionally high in coming years—29 percent—for cement masons and concrete finishers. It should be noted, though, that many of the new jobs will be in highway and bridge construction. For the comparatively small career field of terrazzo work, a 20-percent growth rate is foreseen.

Jobs for tile and marble setters are expected to increase 15 percent by 2022. This is slower than the growth rate in some of the other roofing and flooring sectors but faster than the average for all occupations. Tile, marble, and other natural stones are popular in public office buildings, hospitals, schools, malls, and restaurants. Glass and mosaic tiles also are trending in upscale homes. The best job prospects await tile and marble setters who have experience as well as knowledge in other areas of construction.

In related careers, job growth estimates vary. For example, jobs for cost estimators in all industries are predicted to increase 26 percent by 2022, a dramatic rate of expansion. The need for construction and building inspectors is expected to increase by 12 percent, about the average for all careers.

EMPLOYMENT AND PAY STATISTICS

Roofers held 132,700 jobs in 2012. About 64 percent were employed by roofing contractors. Approximately 28 percent were self-employed. The median pay was $35,290 annually or $16.97 per hour, according to the BLS. Overall, pay for roofers ranged from about $22,000 for entry-level and apprentice workers to more than $60,000 annually for long-time veterans.

Carpenters in all branches of construction held slightly more than 900,000 jobs in 2012. About 36 percent were self-employed. Most self-employed carpenters work in home building. The median wage for carpenters that year was $39,940. Some entry-level carpenters and apprentices earned less than $25,000. Many experienced workers earned more than $70,000.

The median salary for construction laborers and helpers is $29,160. As of 2012, approximately 23 percent of construction laborers worked for themselves; very few helpers are self-employed. Self-employed laborers can accept or reject jobs and establish their own schedules. At the same time, they must handle the business part of their careers. This part includes accounting and taxes. They must have discipline and dedication. If they are lazy, their businesses will stagnate or fail.

As of 2012, approximately 144,300 cement masons and terrazzo workers were employed in the United States. Most worked as specialty trade contractors. Cement masons and concrete finishers earned a median salary of $35,750. The mean salary for terrazzo laborers and finishers was $39,740. The lowest-paid workers in these jobs earned $23,000 or less while the highest-paid earned more than $64,000. The starting pay for apprentices averages about half that of experienced workers.

In 2012, there were 39,200 tile and marble setting jobs in the United States. Most workers were employed by building finishing contractors. Approximately 31 percent were self-employed. Tile and marble setters earn about $37,040 on average.

Demand in coming years will be especially strong for roofers with green roofing experience. In 2012 PV installers who specialize in solar roofing earned median salaries of approximately $37,900.

Salary statistics in related careers are wide-ranging. Cost estimators earned a median annual salary of $58,860 in 2012. The median salary for construction and building inspectors

This example of a green roof is on the Walter Reed Community Center in Arlington, Virginia. Sustainable roofing is gaining momentum.

was $53,450. Sales agents might work for a salary, a commission on sales contracts, or a combination.

A MATTER OF PRIDE

Few things in life are more satisfying than completing a long, demanding task and knowing you did the job well. For workers in some occupations, the job means little more than putting in your hours and drawing your pay. For builders, especially those who construct roofs and floors, the job is much more. They have the privilege of admiring their finished handiwork: a neatly shingled roof or a floor of sturdy hardwood or beautiful mosaic tile.

As BLS statistics show, any of the various occupations related to roofing and flooring pays relatively well and always will be in demand. Best of all, it is a career field in which all workers can take pride.

Roof completed! Nothing in any career is more exhilarating than the celebration of a job that was done well and finished on schedule.

glossary

adhesive A product such as glue or tape used for holding materials in place.

asphalt The composition used in making waterproof shingles as well as roads and other surfaces.

bitumen A mixture of hydrocarbons and nonmetals used for surfacing material.

bonded Insured for damages to property or people that might occur during the performance of one's work.

caulk A material used to make joints and seams watertight.

commission The percentage of a sale amount paid to the sales representative.

compound A construction material, such as a floor coating, composed of multiple substances.

epoxy A type of glue.

equilibrium A sense of balance.

grout Mortar used to fill joints and cracks in masonry.

habitat The natural environment of a particular species of wildlife.

irrigation A system of watering a garden or field.

joist A brace within a framework.

median wage The annual salary or wage in an occupation at which half of the workers earn more and half earn less.

membrane A thin sheet of material that forms a layer of roofing.

mosaic A floor surface made of pieces of material in different colors, sizes, and shapes.

nomad A person or tribe who lives in different places, usually moving as seasons change.

rebar A steel rod with a ridged surface, used to reinforce concrete.

regulation A requirement imposed by a government agency or employer.

renovation The restoration of a deteriorated building or room to its original condition.

scaffold A temporary platform to support workers in elevated places.

sealant Plastic material applied to roofs and floors to keep them waterproof.

shingles Small, thin pieces of building material installed on a roof in an overlapping pattern.

synthetic Artificially made material.

template A basic word processing document on which new documents can be based, such as a résumé.

for more information

Bureau of Labor Statistics (BLS)
2 Massachusetts Avenue NE, Room 2850
Washington, DC 20212
(202) 691-5200
Website: http://www.bls.gov
BLS is a Department of Labor agency that analyzes job descriptions, salaries, growth, demands, trends, and statistics. It publishes the *Occupational Outlook Handbook* (http://www.bls.gov/ooh/) that provides information about hundreds of career fields and specific jobs.

Canadian Roofing Contractors Association (CRCA)
2430 Don Reid Drive, Suite 100
Ottawa, ON K1H 1E1
Canada
(800) 461-2722 or (613) 232-6724
Website: http://www.roofingcanada.com
The CRCA consists of companies engaged in the roofing and related sheet metal contracting business in Canada. It includes companies working in manufacturing or supplying materials and services used in any branch of the roofing and sheet metal industry.

Canadian Standards Association (CSA)
178 Rexdale Boulevard
Toronto, ON M9W 1R3
Canada
(416) 747-4000
Website: http://www.csagroup.org
The CSA Group, chartered in 1919, develops standards for all

Canadian industries, including construction, buildings, and infrastructure.

Home Builders Institute (HBI)
1201 15th Street NW, Sixth Floor
Washington, DC 20005
(800) 795-7955
Website: http://www.hbi.org
Dedicated to career training in the building industry, HBI seeks to prepare students with skills and experience through preapprenticeship training, job placement services, textbooks, mentoring, and other resources.

International Masonry Institute (IMI)
17101 Science Drive
Bowie, MD 20715
(301) 291-2124
Website: http://www.imiweb.org
IMI is an alliance between the International Union of Bricklayers and Allied Craftworkers and their contractors. It offers technical services, research and development, and apprenticeship and training resources.

Mason Contractors Association of America
1481 Merchant Drive
Algonquin, IL 60102
(800) 536-2225 or (224) 678-9709
Website: http://www.masoncontractors.org
The national trade association representing mason contractors promotes the masonry industry with continuing education. It advocates safe work environments and fair codes and standards. It promotes the benefits of masonry materials and assists in the recruitment of workers.

National Roofing Contractors Association
10255 W. Higgins Road, Suite 600
Rosemont, IL 60018-5607
(847) 299-9070
Website: http://www.nrca.net
This nonprofit trade association for roofing professionals was founded in 1886. It represents roofing contractors, manufacturers, distributors, engineers, architects, consultants, building owners, and officials in government agencies.

National Terrazzo and Mosaic Association (NTMA)
P.O. Box 2605
Fredericksburg, TX 78624
(800) 323-9736
Website: http://www.ntma.com
The NTMA establishes national standards for terrazzo floor and wall systems. It provides specifications, color palettes, and general information to architects and designers.

Websites

Because of the changing nature of Internet links, Rosen Publishing has developed an online list of websites related to the subject of this book. This site is updated regularly. Please use this link to access the list:

http://www.rosenlinks.com/ECAR/Roof

for further reading

Bailey, Diane. *Entrepreneurial Smarts* (Get Smart with Your Money). New York, NY: Rosen Publishing, 2013.

Brett, Peter. *Site Carpentry* (Construction NVQ Series Level 2). New York, NY: Oxford University Press, 2014.

Byers, Ann. *Jobs as Green Builders and Planners* (Green Careers). New York, NY: Rosen Publishing, 2010.

Construction (Ferguson's Careers in Focus). 5th ed. New York, NY: Ferguson Publishing, 2010.

Crabtree, Marc. *Meet My Neighbor the Builder.* Saint Catharine's, ON: Crabtree Publishing Company, 2009.

Flath, Camden. *Careers in Green Energy: Fueling the World with Renewable Resources* (New Careers for the 21st Century: Finding Your Role in the Global Renewal). Broomall, PA: Mason Crest Publishers, 2011.

Gerber, Larry. *Top 10 Tips for Developing Money Management Skills* (Tips for Success). New York, NY: Rosen Publishing, 2013.

Jones, Marie. *Top 10 Tips for Planning for a Career* (Tips for Success). New York, NY: Rosen Publishing, 2013.

La Bella, Laura. *Internship & Volunteer Opportunities for People Who Love to Build Things* (Foot in the Door). New York, NY: Rosen Publishing, 2012.

Luckett, Kelly. *Green Roof Construction and Maintenance.* New York, NY: McGraw-Hill, 2009.

McGowan, John. *Complete Do-It-Yourself: An Essential Guide to Painting, Papering, Tiling, Flooring, Woodwork, Shelves and Storage, Home Repairs, Home Insulation, Outdoor Projects and Outdoor Repairs.* London, England: Lorenz Books, 2014.

Miller, Malinda. *Green Construction: Creating Energy-Efficient, Low-Impact Buildings* (New Careers for the 21st Century: Finding Your Role in the Global Renewal). Broomall, PA: Mason Crest Publishers, 2011.

Miller, Mark R., and Rex Miller. *Carpenter's and Builder's Tools, Steel Square & Joinery*. 7th ed. Indianapolis, IN: Wiley, 2005.

Mondschein, Kenneth C. *Construction and Trades* (Great Careers with a High School Diploma). New York, NY: Facts on File, 2008.

Niver, Heather Moore. *Careers in Construction* (Essential Careers). New York, NY: Rosen Classroom, 2013.

Schwartz, Jill C. *Green Careers in Building and Landscaping*. Lawrenceville, NJ: Peterson's, 2010.

Senker, Cath. *Construction Careers* (In the Workplace). Mankato, MN: Amicus, 2010.

Vogt, Floyd, and Gaspar J. Lewis. *Carpentry*. 6th ed. Clifton Park, NY: Delmar Cengage Learning, 2014.

bibliography

Beesley, Caron. "How to Start a Small Construction or General Contracting Business." U.S. Small Business Administration, Starting a Business blog, updated February 18, 2015. Retrieved June 2015 (http://www.sba.gov/blogs/how-start-small-construction-or-general-contracting-business).

Bolles, Mark Emery, and Richard Nelson Bolles. *What Color Is Your Parachute? Guide to Job-Hunting Online*, 6th ed. Berkeley, CA: Ten Speed Press, 2011.

Choice Roof Contractor Group website. "Roofing Tools and Equipment List." Retrieved May 2015 (http://www.choiceroofcontractors.com/roofing-tools-list-for-commercial-roof-contractors).

ContractorTalk.com. "Any Good Roofing Stories?" Retrieved May 2015 (http://www.contractortalk.com/f15/any-good-roofing-stories-1779).

Ferguson's Encyclopedia of Careers and Vocational Guidance. 15th ed., vols. 3 and 5. New York, NY: Infobase Learning, 2011.

HardwoodInstall.com. "Hardwood Flooring Tools." Retrieved May 2015 (http://www.hardwoodinstaller.com/tools/general.htm).

Lindus Construction. "Re-roofing: Installation Process." YouTube video, "Today's Home Remodeler" series, February 19, 2011. Retrieved June 2015 (http://www.youtube.com/watch?v=ERoFfk_bQhs).

Miller, Mark J. "A Farm Grows in Brooklyn—on the Roof." *National Geographic*, April 29, 2014.

Parks, Barbara, and Jodi Helmer. *The Complete Idiot's Guide to Green Careers*. New York, NY: Alpha Books (Penguin Group), 2009.

Perrotta, Tom. "Slowly, a Roof Rises Over Arthur Ashe Stadium in Queens." *Wall Street Journal*, May 6, 2015. Retrieved June 2015 (http://www.wsj.com/articles/slowly-a-roof-rises-over-arthur-ashe-stadium-in-queens-1430906401).

Roofrepairstore. "Topseal Fibreglass Roof Installation." YouTube video, September 17, 2011. Retrieved June 2015 (http://www.youtube.com/watch?v=lbbe4PnEGRY).

Shatkin, Laurence. *150 Best Jobs for Your Skills*. 2nd ed. St. Paul, MN: JIST Publishing, 2012.

Shatkin, Laurence. *300 Best Jobs Without a Four-Year Degree*, 4th ed. St. Paul, MN: JIST Publishing, 2013.

Tuttiett, Philippa. "How to Lay Vinyl or Lino Flooring." YouTube video, May 23, 2013. Retrieved June 2015 (http://www.youtube.com/watch?v=i9S7z_8QWc0).

U.S. Department of Labor, Bureau of Labor Statistics. *Occupational Outlook Handbook*. Retrieved March 2015 (http://www.bls.gov/ooh).

Vila, Bob. "Asphalt Roof Shingles Installation." YouTube video, March 30, 2015. Retrieved June 2015 (http://www.youtube.com/watch?v=iaDop-7F6Bc).

Waltz, Nicholas J. "Roof Taking Shape Around Arthur Ashe Stadium." U.S. Open 2015 website, November 21, 2014. Retrieved June 2015 (http://www.usopen.org/news/roof_taking_shape_around_arthur_ashe_stadium).

index